First World War
and Army of Occupation
War Diary
France, Belgium and Germany

1 INDIAN CAVALRY DIVISION
Lucknow Cavalry Brigade,
Brigade Signal Troop
3 August 1914 - 31 December 1916

WO95/1175/3

The Naval & Military Press Ltd
www.nmarchive.com
Published in association with The National Archives

Published by

The Naval & Military Press Ltd

Unit 10 Ridgewood Industrial Park,

Uckfield, East Sussex,

TN22 5QE England

Tel: +44 (0) 1825 749494

www.naval-military-press.com

www.nmarchive.com

This diary has been reprinted in facsimile from the original. Any imperfections are inevitably reproduced and the quality may fall short of modern type and cartographic standards.

© **Crown Copyright**
Images reproduced by permission of The National Archives, London, England, 2015.

Contents

Document type	Place/Title	Date From	Date To
Heading	WO95/1175-3		
Heading	BEF 1 Ind Cav. Div. Lucknow Bde Lucknow Bde Signal Troop 1914 Aug To 1916 Dec		
Heading	War Diary of Signal Troop Lucknow Cavy. Brigade From 3-8-14 To 31-12-14		
War Diary	Lucknow	03/08/1914	10/09/1914
War Diary	Orleans	24/11/1917	07/12/1917
War Diary	Lillers	10/12/1917	15/12/1917
War Diary	Norrent Fontes	22/12/1917	25/12/1917
War Diary	Heuchin	26/12/1917	31/12/1917
Heading	War Diary of Lucknow Brigade Signal Troop. From. 1st January 1915 To 31st January 1915		
War Diary	Heuchin	01/01/1915	09/01/1915
War Diary	Festubert	10/01/1915	11/01/1915
War Diary	Heuchin	12/01/1915	31/01/1915
Heading	War Diary of Lucknow Cavalry Brigade, Signal Troop. From 1st. March 1915. To 31st. March 1915		
War Diary	Heuchin	01/03/1915	07/03/1915
War Diary	Febvin	08/03/1915	11/03/1915
War Diary	Marles	12/03/1915	12/03/1915
War Diary	Auchel	13/03/1915	14/03/1915
War Diary	Febvin	15/03/1915	16/03/1915
War Diary	Ligny-Les-Aire	17/03/1915	18/03/1915
War Diary	Liettres	19/03/1915	31/03/1915
Heading	War Diary of Lucknow Cavalry Brigade Signal Troop. From 1st April 1915 To 30 April 1915		
War Diary	Liettres	01/04/1915	24/04/1915
War Diary	Cassel	25/04/1915	28/04/1915
War Diary	St Jans Ter Beigen	29/04/1915	30/04/1915
Heading	War Diary of Lucknow Cavalry Brigade Signal Troop. From 1st. May 1915 To 31st. May 1915		
War Diary	St. Jans Ter Biezen	01/05/1915	02/05/1915
War Diary	Cassel	03/05/1915	05/05/1915
War Diary	Mametz	06/05/1915	17/05/1915
War Diary	Le Reveillon	18/05/1915	18/05/1915
War Diary	Burbure	19/05/1915	27/05/1915
War Diary	Oxelaire	28/05/1915	28/05/1915
War Diary	L'Erklesbrugge	28/05/1915	28/05/1915
War Diary	Vlamertinghe	29/05/1915	31/05/1915
Heading	War Diary of Lucknow Cavalry Brigade. Signal Troop. From. 1st. June 1915 To 30th June. 1915		
War Diary	Vlamertinge	01/06/1915	02/06/1915
War Diary	Ypres Salient	03/06/1915	05/06/1915
War Diary	Vlamertinge	06/05/1915	14/05/1915
War Diary	Mametz	15/05/1915	30/05/1915
Heading	War Diary of Signal Troop, Lucknow Cavalry Brigade. From 1st July 1915 To 31st August 1915		
War Diary	Mametz	01/07/1915	05/08/1915
War Diary	Berteaucourt	06/08/1915	07/08/1915
War Diary	Canaples	08/08/1915	23/08/1915

War Diary	Authville	24/08/1915	31/08/1915
Heading	War Diary of Signal Troop Lucknow Cavalry Brigade From 1st September 1915 To 31st October 1915		
War Diary	Authville	01/09/1915	02/09/1915
War Diary	Bernueil	03/09/1915	08/09/1915
War Diary	St Leger	09/09/1915	10/09/1915
War Diary	Behencourt	11/09/1915	11/09/1915
War Diary	Authville	12/09/1915	14/09/1915
War Diary	Trenches	15/09/1915	17/09/1915
War Diary	St Leger	17/09/1915	22/09/1915
War Diary	Mon Plaisir	23/09/1915	24/10/1915
War Diary	Cavillon	26/10/1915	31/10/1915
Heading	War Diary of Signal Troop Lucknow Cavalry Brigade. From 1st November 1915 To 31st December 1915		
War Diary	Cavillon	01/11/1915	17/11/1915
War Diary	Vieulaine	18/11/1915	15/12/1915
War Diary	Franleu	16/12/1915	31/12/1915
Heading	War Diary of Signal Troop Lucknow Cavalry Brigade From 1st July 1916 To 31st July 1916		
War Diary	Grouches	01/07/1915	01/07/1915
War Diary	March	02/07/1915	02/07/1915
War Diary	Frohen-Le-Grand	03/07/1915	19/07/1915
War Diary	March	19/07/1915	19/07/1915
War Diary	Villers Brulin	20/07/1915	30/07/1915
War Diary	March	30/07/1915	30/07/1915
Heading	War Diary of Signal Troop Lucknow Cavalry Brigade From 1st August 1916 To 31st August 1916		
War Diary	Chelers	01/08/1916	08/08/1916
War Diary	March	09/08/1916	09/08/1916
War Diary	Pas	10/08/1916	31/08/1916
Heading	War Diary of Signal Troop Lucknow Cavalry Brigade From 1st September 1916 To 30th September 1916		
War Diary	Pas	01/09/1916	01/09/1916
War Diary	March	03/09/1916	23/09/1916
War Diary	Morlencourt	27/09/1916	30/09/1916
Heading	War Diary of Signal Troop Lucknow Cavalry Brigade From 1st October 1916 To 30th November 1916		
War Diary	Crecy	01/10/1916	01/11/1916
War Diary	Moyenneville	02/11/1916	30/11/1916
Heading	War Diary of Signal Troop Lucknow Cavalry Brigade From 1st December 1916 To 31st December 1916		
Heading	War Diary. of Lucknow Cavalry Brigade Signal Troop. For the Month of December, 1916		
War Diary	Moyenneville	01/12/1916	31/12/1916

WO 95/11757/3

BEF

1 Ind Cav. Div.

Lucknow Bde

Lucknow Bde Signal Troop
1914 Aug to 1916 Dec

WAR DIARY

of

Signal Troop Lucknow Cav_y. Brigade

from 3-8-14 To 31-12-14.

Army Form C. 2118.

WAR DIARY
or
INTELLIGENCE SUMMARY.

(Erase heading not required.)

Instructions regarding War Diaries and Intelligence Summaries are contained in F. S. Regs., Part II, and the Staff Manual respectively. Title pages will be prepared in manuscript.

ADJUTANT GENERAL INDIA
28. JAN. 1915

Hour. Date, Place.	Summary of Events and Information.	Remarks and references to Appendices.
3rd August 1914. Lucknow	Order for mobilization and formation of Signal Troop received. Equipment indents for.	
10 Sept. 1914. Lucknow	Equipment received (Training) & prepared for journey, in charge of R.S.E.	
24th November. Orleans	Signal troop formed from units of 11th Lancers, 29th Lancers, & 36th Jacob's Horse.	
26 do. Orleans	Troops move into a Camp of its own.	
7th December. Orleans	Signal Troop entrained with 1st Light H.Q. at 2.15 a.m. on night of 7-8 December. No casualties on the journey.	
10th December. Lillers	Troop arrives & went into billets at Lillers. Native units have out in open.	
15th December. Villers	Native units in the Troop changed their horses into (open). Went into good billets in the fields in Ready to move.	

SA

WAR DIARY
or
INTELLIGENCE SUMMARY.
(Erase heading not required.)

Army Form C. 2118.

Instructions regarding War Diaries and Intelligence Summaries are contained in F. S. Regs., Part II, and the Staff Manual respectively. Title pages will be prepared in manuscript.

Hour. Date. Place.	Summary of Events and Information.	Remarks and references to Appendices.
15th December Illies	Had curus with all outlying units (29th & 86th) by lamp from Church tower by night. Aeroplane rifle by day. Sialkote Bde. joined us again up with us	
22nd December Morrent Fontes	Marched to MORRENT-FONTES at 7:30 am & went into billets there. Good accommodation	
23rd do. do.	Ran a line to 29th at Saint Hilaire & 36th to them.	
25th do. do.	Marched with brigade to SEVELIN leaving to man. Picked up telephone wire.	
26th do. Sevelin	Ran a line to 29th at FONTAINE-LEZ-BOUVARYS from them to 36th at PREDEFIN & they ran a line to HQrs at LISBOURG.	
31st do. do.	Ran a separate line to HQrs at LISBOURG.	

WAR DIARY

OF

Lucknow Brigade Signal Troop.

From 1st January 1915 To 31st January 1915

121/44101

Army Form C. 2118.

WAR DIARY
or
INTELLIGENCE SUMMARY

(Erase heading not required.)

Instructions regarding War Diaries and Intelligence Summaries are contained in F. S. Regs., Part II. and the Staff Manual respectively. Title pages will be prepared in manuscript.

Hour. Date. Place.	Summary of Events and Information.	Remarks and references to Appendices.
January 1915 Hénencourt	Remained in billets. No change. Wires frequently cut.	
9 Jan. do.	Orders to be ready for 48 hours. Fell in trenches. Went by motor bus to BETHUNE & on foot to FESTUBERT. On arrival there relieve the Argyllses of Seaforths. Took up Battalion Head Quarters line forty. All wires cut except on north of 9-10, but wire to trenches cut in early morning, but it was too late to mend on account of the day light.	
10 Jan. Festubert.	Note from 12 B.g. Head Quarters to 36 Head Quarters. Cut. Mended it. That wire wire mending party passed wire towards trenches & found no measuring rods out at the trenches & join to measuring rods one at the trenches. Broken in twelve had even in wire the trenches. Broken in twelve but mended again. Rest of wires are good.	WTB

Army Form C. 2118.

WAR DIARY
or
INTELLIGENCE SUMMARY.
(Erase heading not required.)

Instructions regarding War Diaries and Intelligence Summaries are contained in F. S. Regs., Part II, and the Staff Manual respectively. Title pages will be prepared in manuscript.

Hour. Date. Place.	Summary of Events and Information.	Remarks and references to Appendices.

11 Jan 1915 Festubert — Line quiet already, but withdrawal of troops from front line. Line drawn of Cable & Telephone lost in water of trench. Hanson over to M H on Signal Troop about 7 p.m. rather rough journey under to BETHUNE. Line by Telephone good the whole time during spell in trenches with the exception of some breaks which been at once mended & not being able to running line to trenches on 10th day time.

12 Jan Hinges — Arrived back at base.

14th Jan. do. — Reconnaissance up with dist. Rifle Brigade. Line good.

15 do. — Line out with field Rite Rifle Bde. line mended

18 do. — Inspection by C. in C.

21st do. — Ordinary work mainly connection of wounded line & putting in new lines.

Army Form C. 2118.

WAR DIARY
or
INTELLIGENCE SUMMARY.
(Erase heading not required.)

Instructions regarding War Diaries and Intelligence Summaries are contained in F. S. Regs., Part II, and the Staff Manual respectively. Title pages will be prepared in manuscript.

Hour. Date. Place.	Summary of Events and Information.	Remarks and references to Appendices.
27 Jan. Heneka.	Ordinary work has gone on for the last 3 days. Severe recruiting parades, trenching. Telephone wires etc.	
30 Jan. Heneka.	Received orders to stand to, to harass enemy known at an hour notice. New Khaki lamps arrived.	
31 Jan. Heneka.	Heavy fall of snow. Several wires broken. Resumed new lamps started then.	off.

WAR DIARY

Lucknow Cavalry Brigade, Signal Troop.

From 1st March 1915. 31st March 1915

Army Form O. 2118

Lucknow Cavalry Brigade Signal Troop

WAR DIARY
or
INTELLIGENCE SUMMARY.
(Erase heading not required.)

Instructions regarding War Diaries and Intelligence Summaries are contained in F. S. Regs., Part II, and the Staff Manual respectively. Title pages will be prepared in manuscript.

ADJUTANT GENERAL
-5. APR 1915
1294 W.P.
BASE OFFICE

Hour. Date, Place.	Summary of Events and Information.	Remarks and references to Appendices.
March 1st Meerut	Signalling practice & Exercise	
2nd "	Exercise. Regiments of Bde digging reserve trenches at Roberg.	
3rd "		
4th "	Exercise, and Signalling (Visual) practice	
5th "		
6th "	Divisional Day under Bde. Commander. Bde split up in two parts one part forming enemy.	
7th "	Exercise, saddle room inspection in afternoon. Lamp Signalling at night. Exercise in morning. At 3.30 P.M. Received orders to move the clerk & kittle by 6.30 P.M. arrived Jeherum at 8.30 P.M. Laid wires from Sialkot Bde to own H.Q.	
8th Jeherum	No exercise standing by to move practically at moments notice.	
9th "	Short exercise.	
10th "	Short exercise, repairing wires. Laying wires fat way to 36 J. Horse	
11th "	Received orders to move at 9AM. Stood to all day moved 3AM next morning	
12th Marlea	Moved at 3.30 A.M. arrived at Marlea 6-7 miles 9AM. Transport arrived about 4.30 P.M.	
	Troop moved at 11:30 AM. Bde followed at 1 P.M. Arrived Andhel about 1 P.M. Lapped in on a line to Jeherum. 29th & 36 J. Horse quite close. Nothing	
13th Andhel	Exercise round hertel square. Standing to, to move at an hours notice.	
14th "	Short Exercise. Moved at 6.30 P.M. back to Jeherum arriving at 8.30 P.M.	

Major
Captain

Lucknow Bde. Signal Troop. Army Form C. 2118

WAR DIARY
or
INTELLIGENCE SUMMARY.

(Erase heading not required.)

Hour. Date. Place.	Summary of Events and Information.	Remarks and references to Appendices.
Tehran. 15th March	Reconnre, relating wires to K.D.Col. 190ft Lines at Shekin. Standing to.	
" 16th "	Moved from Tehran to Jejin-bar-Ore at 10 am arriving about 11.30 AM. Lines laid back to Yaro & Shekin & to Bde HQ	
Jejin-bar-Ore 17th "	Reconnre. Notice to move increased to 4 hours.	
" 18th "	Moved at 9.15 am to Lietties arrived about 10.30 am. Rest of day in getting wires ready to lay.	
Lietties 19th "	Reconnre. Standing to still. Wires laid to Bde HQ at Lequin also to Sqdn & 36th J. Horse	
" 20th "	Reconnre. Arranging for lines for horses outside.	
" 21st "	Reconnre. Parties renewing & testing wires. Telephone reading practice.	
" 22nd "	Reconnre. Feeling on wire left at Jebron Lequin-tes-Ore.	
" 23 to 30 "	Reconnre. & practice Telephone reading. Notice to move increased to 6 hours.	
" 31st "	Brigade Training. Bde split into two parts, one forming an attacking party.	

W. Marsh - Captain
Cmg. Lucknow Cavalry Bde Signal Troop

121/5504   General No 239

WAR DIARY
OF
Lucknow Cavalry Brigade Signal Troop.

From 1st April 1915 To 30th April 1915

Army Form C. 2118.

WAR DIARY
or
INTELLIGENCE SUMMARY. Jukhusi Bambay Bde Signal Troop
(Erase heading not required.)

April 1915.

Instructions regarding War Diaries and Intelligence Summaries are contained in F. S. Regs., Part II, and the Staff Manual respectively. Title pages will be prepared in manuscript.

Hour. Date. Place.	Summary of Events and Information.	Remarks and references to Appendices.
Jukhusi 1st April 1915	Exercise, class for native sigrs. on telephone.	
2nd "	Bde training. Signal troop opht with each regiment	
3rd "	Exercise, signalling practice transmission flags.	
4th	Exercise, standing to.	
5th	Exercise. Natives in buggery class in afternoon.	
6th	Exercise. signalling practice. Revolver practice	
7th		
8th		
9th	Exercise + signalling practice.	
10th		
11th	Exercise. Horse show in afternoon. Jumping &c	
	Exercise. Native soldiers finish competing for jumping	
13th	Exercise. Flag transmission work in afternoon	
15th	Troop Dull under O/c Sig. Troop. Bungey class in afternoon	W. Maut

Army Form C. 2118.

WAR DIARY
or
INTELLIGENCE SUMMARY.

Lucknow Bde Signal Troop.

April 1915.

(Erase heading not required.)

Instructions regarding War Diaries and Intelligence Summaries are contained in F. S. Regs., Part II, and the Staff Manual respectively. Title pages will be prepared in manuscript.

Hour. Date, Place.	Summary of Events and Information.	Remarks and references to Appendices.
Littre 14th April 1915	Exercise. Signalling practice.	
15th "	Parade at Hinxbie for prize photographs &c. Been parade.	
16th "	Exercise. Buzzing class in afternoon. Jump Cow: with recent Bde at night from road mines	
17th "	Exercise. Signalling practice. One m/c D.R. went to Rue Cardeure with despatch. at Thelinelles	
18th "	Exercise. Signalling practice. One m/c D.R. proceeded on special duty	
19th "	Riding school jumping.	
20th "	Exercise.	
21st " 22nd " 23rd "	Bde on trench digging at Robecq. One m/c D.R. went to Boulogne on despatch.	
⟨ 24th ⟩ 25	— " — — " —	
	Orders received for a move at 2 hours notice. Move about 6.30 P.M. arrived in the morning of the 25th at 4.10 A.M. Route - Busnes, through or the night, Hinges in fact then in baron. Quinines Bertinham Cassel.	
Cassel 26th ⟩ 27th 28th ⟩	Awaiting to move at any notice. Short exercise.	
	Moved at 1 P.M. to St Jan ter Biezen arrived 4.30 P.M. Ran into B.E.F (Cavalry)	W May-

Army Form C. 2118.

WAR DIARY
or
INTELLIGENCE SUMMARY.

(Erase heading not required.)

Lucknow Brigade Signal Troop

April 1915

Hour. Date. Place.	Summary of Events and Information.	Remarks and references to Appendices.
At Jam ti Bergen. 29 April 30"	About sixreen, still standing to at a moments notice. "Do"	

Waugh -
Captain
Lucknow Brigade Signal Troop

Maj.
Lucknow Brigade

Serial No 239.

WAR DIARY
OF
Lucknow Cavalry Brigade Signal Troop.

From 1st May 1915 TO 31st May 1915.

Army Form C. 2118.

WAR DIARY
or
INTELLIGENCE SUMMARY. Lucknow Cavalry Brigade Signal Troop
(Erase heading not required.)

Instructions regarding War Diaries and Intelligence Summaries are contained in F. S. Regs., Part II. and the Staff Manual respectively. Title pages will be prepared in manuscript.

Hour, Date, Place	Summary of Events and Information	Remarks and references to Appendices
St Jean de Bezu. 1st May 1915.	Short exercise, received next to move by 6AM next day	
" " 2nd " "	Left at 6AM for Cassel arrived about 10.A.M.	
Cassel 3rd " "	Standing to expecting to move at any moment	
" 4th " "	Received orders to move to night. Move at 1AM.	
" 5th " "	Left Cassel at 1AM for Momely arrived about 5.30 a.m.	
Momely 6th " "	Exercises. Under four hours notice to move.	
" 7th " "	Lances on buggy class in afternoon.	
" 8th " "	Exercise. Stables in buggy class in afternoon.	
" 9th " "	Exercise & paying in afternoon. Was under 2 hours notice to move.	
" 10th " "	Exercise. Buggying class & field stables in afternoon. Rain at night	
" 11th " "	Exercise. Arm inspection equipment. Buggying class. More rain.	
" 12th " "		
" 13th " "	Exercise & buggying classes also grazing in afternoon	
" 14th " "		
" 15th " "		
" 16th " "	No exercise, expect to move. Packing up.	

Army Form C. 2118.

WAR DIARY
or
INTELLIGENCE SUMMARY.
(Erase heading not required.) Lucknow Cavalry Brigade Signal Troop.

Instructions regarding War Diaries and Intelligence Summaries are contained in F.S. Regs., Part II. and the Staff Manual respectively. Title pages will be prepared in manuscript.

Hour, Date, Place	Summary of Events and Information	Remarks and references to Appendices
March 17th May 1915. Le Revillon	Orders received to move at 3 P.M. Moved at 3.45 P.M. to Le Revillon	
" 18th "	Arrived at at 7.45 P.M. last night. Move to Burbure to day	
Burbure 19th "	Arrived here about noon.	
" 20th "	Received orders to go back to original billets. Left about 12 noon arrived Neuvilly at 5 P.M.	
" 21st "	Four hours notice. Neuvivis	
" 22nd "	Staff ride signalling scheme with Genl. staff & Regtl. Signallers	
" 23rd "	Went to rifle range at Fiefries for rifle practice.	
" 24th "	Received. Bugging class in afternoon.	
" 25th "	Brigade staff ride communication scheme over same ground as before	
" 26th "	Swimming lessons in river. News of joining 2nd Army.	
" 27th "	Moved from Neuvivis at 9 A.M. to Oultaine arriving about 4.30 P.M.	
Oultaine 28th "	Left here about 5 A.M. for L'Rhkleshugge reached there about 9 A.M.	
L'Rhkleshugge 28th "	Left at 2 P.M. in motor buses for Vlamertinghe arriving 5 P.M.	
Vlamertinghe 29th "	Moved Bde. Head Qrs into the Town. Several rifle burst on Pofcenighe & Vlamertinghe road	Abbage - Baston. O/c Lucknow Bde Signal Troop.
" 30th "	Established communication between Brigades & Divisions. Much heavy firing to N.E	
" 31st "	Men went on route march for exercise. Shell struck house behind a hospital killing 2 & causing small injuries from debris	

WAR DIARY

Lucknow Cavalry Brigade Signal Troop.

From 1st June 1915 to 30th June 1915.

WAR DIARY or INTELLIGENCE SUMMARY

Army Form C. 2118.

Lucknow Cav Brigade
Ending June 30 1915

(Erase heading not required.)

Hour, Date, Place	Summary of Events and Information	Remarks and references to Appendices
1. 10.15 pm 1st June VLAMERTINGE	In telephone cne with Division – 4½ miles in rear – KDGs went to find line trenches under 3rd Bn. Telephone cne impossible account of shell fire.	
2. 9 pm 2nd June VLAMERTINGE	Wires in communication with 3rd Cav Bde taken up one matches also with 2nd Cav Div – in afternoon – trench digging	No 3 Section A.G's Office at Base I.E. Force Passed to 4. 7. S. Sect on 15
3. am 3rd June YPRES-SALIENT	The Ypres salient in reserve trenches HQ in dug outs	
3. " 4 June "	Got into our position by comn communication with 36th (Bagganies advanced) with 29th and 3rd Cav don (Scots) 2 of Jacobs H wounded – no casualties among signallers line had to be mended 4 times through the night under fire – at no time did communication break down for more than ½ hour.	
10 pm 5 June "	In dug out & trenches all day under shrapnel fire communications intact left trenches 10.30	
1 am 6 June VLAMERTINGE	Arrived VLAMERTINGE 1 am – no further casualties –	
10 " 7 " "	Telephone cme with one div & 3rd Cav Div. DRT regiment 29 lines shelled 2 animals killed	

Army Form C. 2118.

WAR DIARY
or
INTELLIGENCE SUMMARY.

(Erase heading not required.)

Instructions regarding War Diaries and Intelligence
Summaries are contained in F.S. Regs., Part II.
and the Staff Manual respectively. Title pages
will be prepared in manuscript.

Hour, Date, Place	Summary of Events and Information	Remarks and references to Appendices
8th June VERMERTINGE	29 Lancers near Klut.	
9 " "	no change. KDG Signs Barges fracin	
10 " "	Village shelled. Barges intelligence	
	Casualties engaged in putting out fires in houses & cars	
	successful	
11 " "	no change	Buggin
12 " "	"	Buggin
13 " "		Buggin
14 " "	Shells heard casualties in Division	
15 " MAMETZ	Bde ordered 7 am reached Billeting area 10 am	
	4 Hussars Coys bn had line to Gier & ROCETOIRE	
	KDG & RING. 29th at MAMETZ, 7/6th at MARTHES	
16 " "	Cries with regt by DR	
	Routine work afternoon buggin	
17 " "	"	surveying
18 " "	"	buggin
19 " "	"	grazing

Army Form C. 2118.

WAR DIARY
or
INTELLIGENCE SUMMARY.
(Erase heading not required.)

Instructions regarding War Diaries and Intelligence Summaries are contained in F.S. Regs., Part II. and the Staff Manual respectively. Title pages will be prepared in manuscript.

Hour, Date, Place	Summary of Events and Information	Remarks and references to Appendices
20th June MAMETZ	Nothing routine work grazing to horses	
21. "	" buzzer	
22. "	" buzzer	
23. "	" map reading buzzer lamps	
24. "	" flag grazing	
25. "	" buzzer	
26. "	" heliograph dismounting	
27. "	" grazing	
28. "	" lamp	
29. "	" flag & helio	
30. "	" buzzer	

Vivian Dsarge Capt
O.C. Signal Troop
Lucknow Cavalry Brigade

Serial No 239

WAR DIARY
OF
Signal Troop, Lucknow Cavalry Brigade.

From 1st July 1915 To 31st August 1915

Army Form C. 2118.

WAR DIARY
or
INTELLIGENCE SUMMARY.
Lucknow Cav Brigade ending July 31st (9.15.)

(Erase heading not required.)

Hour, Date, Place	Summary of Events and Information	Remarks and references to Appendices
1st July 1915 MAMETZ	No clears. Routine work. Average of messages sent & received 65/per month.	
2nd July 1915 "	Camp for 2nd class	
3. " "	Routine work. Buzzer kit, saddle & rifle inspection	
	" Buzzer + screen parade	
4 July 1915	Went on staff ride to discuss the squadn' part	
5 " "	Buzzer	
6 " "	helio and flag	
7 " "	buzzer	
8 " "	laying telephone wire + practicing with commutators	
9 " "	buzzer	
10 " "	camp. grazing	
11 " "	flag	
12 " "	helio. grazing	
13 " "	Staff ride with regimental signallers	
14 " "	camp with regimental signallers	
	grazing & horse inspection	

Army Form C. 2118.

WAR DIARY
or
INTELLIGENCE SUMMARY.
(Erase heading not required.)

Lucknow Cav. Bde.
Meerut July 31st 1915

Instructions regarding War Diaries and Intelligence Summaries are contained in F.S. Regs., Part II. and the Staff Manual respectively. Title pages will be prepared in manuscript.

Hour, Date, Place	Summary of Events and Information	Remarks and references to Appendices
15 July 1915	No change. Routine work — officers class of 4 stations.	
16	" " buzzer practice.	
17	" " helio & flag.	
18	" " air line practice in layout.	
19	" " Camp.	
20	" " Staff ride with regtl. sigs.	
21	" " buzzer.	
22	" " helio – Vet inspection.	
23	" " grazing.	
24	" " "	
25	" " Camp.	
26	" " helio.	
27	" " buzzer.	
28	" " grazing.	
29	" " buzzer.	
30	" " Kit inspection.	
31		

Kenneth Douge
Capt
15th Bde. O.C. Signal Troop.

WAR DIARY
or
INTELLIGENCE SUMMARY. Lucknow Cav. Bde.
(Erase heading not required.) ending Aug. 31st 1915

Army Form C. 2118.

Instructions regarding War Diaries and Intelligence Summaries are contained in F. S. Regs., Part II. and the Staff Manual respectively. Title pages will be prepared in manuscript.

Hour, Date, Place		Summary of Events and Information	Remarks and references to Appendices
1st August 1915		Moved to FRUGES	
2nd "		Marched to MARLES QUEL	
3rd "		" " HOUDENCOURT	
4th "		" " BERTEAUCOURT	
5th "		Men sent out in parties of four to reconnoitre surrounding country.	
6th "	BERTEAUCOURT	Routine: cleaning saddlery &c.	
7th "		Moved to CANAPLES.	
8th "	CANAPLES	Routine: assisted Divsn. to lay cable from DOMART to CANAPLES	
9th "	"	Routine.	
10th "	"	ditto	
11th "	"	ditto	
12th "	"	ditto	
13th "	"	Capt. Mackintosh 6th Cavalry, took over command of the Troop.	
14th "	"	No change. Routine work.	
15th "	"	ditto	
16th "	"	ditto. Assisted Divsn. to lay airline from DOMART to CANAPLES, & took in cable.	

Army Form C. 2118.

WAR DIARY
or
INTELLIGENCE SUMMARY.
(Erase heading not required.)

Lucknow Cav Bde
Ending Aug 31st 1915

Hour, Date, Place	Summary of Events and Information	Remarks and references to Appendices
17th August 1915 CANAPLES	No change: Routine	
18— "	ditto	
19— "	ditto	
20— "	ditto	
21— "	ditto.	
22nd — "	Marched to FORCEVILLE at 3 p.m. arriving 11 p.m. Proceeded for night in wood: led horses returning at noon to BEAUCOURT	
23rd — "		
24— " AUTHUILLE	7 a.m. Marched on foot to AUTHUILLE + took over G section signal office. Brigade marched in nights of 23rd—24th. relief completed 12.40 a.m.	
25— "	Livermin made themselves acquainted with all lines.	
26— "	Relay Runners organised for use in case lines became dis.	
27— "	Routine: Relay Runners practised.	
28— "	ditto	
29— "	ditto	
30— "	ditto	
31— "	ditto.	

121/7601

Serial No. 239

Confidential

War Diary

of

Signal Troop, Lucknow Cavalry Brigade.

FROM 1st September 1915 **TO** 31st October 1915

Army Form C. 2118.

WAR DIARY
or
INTELLIGENCE SUMMARY.

(Erase heading not required.)

Signal Troop
1st Anzac Corps
for week ending 30.9.15"

Instructions regarding War Diaries and Intelligence Summaries are contained in F.S. Regs., Part II. and the Staff Manual respectively. Title pages will be prepared in manuscript.

Hour, Date, Place		Summary of Events and Information	Remarks and references to Appendices
September 1st 1915	Authuille	Routine: no change.	
" 2nd	"	Brigade relieved. Signal Troop marches on foot to FORCEVILLE (horses) & trans: rode back to BERNEUIL arriving 3 a.m. on 3rd	
" 3rd	BERNEUIL	Routine; cleaning, bedding kits &c.	
" 4th	"	do	
" 5th	"	do	
" 6th	"	do	
" 7th	"	do	
" 8th	"	do	
" 9th	St LEGER	Moved billets to St Leger; found cable already laid to Division. My Brigade & Brigade Sn were there previously.	
" 10th	"	Routine.	
" 11th	BEHENCOURT	Marched to BEHENCOURT + billeted there for night.	
" 12th	AUTHUILLE	Marched 4 p.m. to near MARTINSART, thence on foot to AUTHUILLE taking over Brigade Sigs. + Brigade office.	
" 13th	"	Routine: Cpl Freemantle killed at Brigade desk.	
" 14th	"	Moved up to G1 Instructor Signal office, being relieved at AUTHUILLE by Australia Divn Signal Troop.	

Army Form C. 2118.

WAR DIARY
or
INTELLIGENCE SUMMARY.
(Erase heading not required.)

Signal Troop.
Lucknow Cav. Bde.
for month ending 30.9.15

Instructions regarding War Diaries and Intelligence Summaries are contained in F. S. Regs., Part II. and the Staff Manual respectively. Title pages will be prepared in manuscript.

Hour, Date, Place		Summary of Events and Information	Remarks and references to Appendices
September 15	1915 Trenches	Lucknow made themselves acquainted with lines.	
" 16	"	Routine. Brigade relieved at night. Signal Troop marched to FOREEVILLE wood, where led horses arrived. Interpreter stance rode to FRESCHENCOURT arriving 3 a.m. 17th	
" 17	ST. LEGER	11.30 a.m. Marched back to billets at ST. LEGER arriving 4 p.m.	
" 18	"	Routine ; cleaning saddlery &c.	
" 19	"	Office routine changes ; utility of 4 hours opened same as instead of 2½ hours refit as previously.	
" 20	"	was done in trenches. Divisional Staff Ride.	
" 21	"	Divisional Field Day ; followed by review by H.E. Lord Kitchener.	
" 22	"	Moved to MON PLAISIR, arriving 5 p.m.	
" 23	MON PLAISIR	Routine ; inspection of rifles, swords, saddlery &c.	
" 24	"	Routine ; inspection of news kits; No. 7 munges 163.	
" 25	"	Routine ; Brigade on one hour notice from 5 a.m. No. 7 munges	
		dealt with 164 ; all by Despatch Riders.	
" 26	"	Routine ; Brigade on 2½ hour notice to move.	

Army Form C. 2118.

WAR DIARY
or
INTELLIGENCE SUMMARY

Spest Troops
Lucknow Cav. Bde.
for month ending 30.9.15

(Erase heading not required.)

Instructions regarding War Diaries and Intelligence Summaries are contained in F.S. Regs., Part II. and the Staff Manual respectively. Title pages will be prepared in manuscript.

Hour, Date, Place	Summary of Events and Information	Remarks and references to Appendices
September 27th MON PLAISIR	Routine: Brigade still on 2½ hours notice to move.	
" 28th "	ditto	
" 29th "	do do	
" 30th "	do do	

Army Form C. 2118.

WAR DIARY
or
INTELLIGENCE SUMMARY.

Signal Troop
Lucknow Cav. Bde.
for month of Sept. 31·X·15

(Erase heading not required.)

Instructions regarding War Diaries and Intelligence Summaries are contained in F.S. Regs., Part II. and the Staff Manual respectively. Title pages will be prepared in manuscript.

Hour, Date, Place	Summary of Events and Information	Remarks and references to Appendices
Oct. 1st MON PLAISIR	Divisional Field day. Troop paraded 8·15 am returned to billets	
" 2 "	6·15 pm managed to feed at mid-day but no water until 5 pm.	
" 3 "	Routine. one cart horse so unsteady it unfit for field.	
" 4 "	ditto	
" 5 "	ditto	
" 5 "	Divisional Field day. Troop paraded 8 am. returned to billets 5 pm: difficulty in getting orderlies to troop H.Q. to report centre quick enough to advance	
" 6 "	Routine	
" 7 "	ditto	
" 8 "	Divisional Field day. Troop paraded 8·15 am returned to billets 5 pm: work much more satisfactory	
" 9 "	Routine	
" 10 "	do	
" 11 "	Brigade Field day.	

WAR DIARY
or
INTELLIGENCE SUMMARY.

(Erase heading not required.)

Army Form C. 2118.

Instructions regarding War Diaries and Intelligence Summaries are contained in F.S. Regs., Part II. and the Staff Manual respectively. Title pages will be prepared in manuscript.

Hour, Date, Place	Summary of Events and Information	Remarks and references to Appendices
Oct. 12. 1915 MON PLAISIR	Routine	
" 13 "	Routine	
" 14 "	"	
" 15 "	Divisional Field day.	
" 16 "	Arranged billeting area from MONT PLAISIR to BERNAVILLE I.C. E. K.D.G. & 2B.S.H. relieved though exchange to Division	
" 17 at DOMART		
" 18 "	Routine.	
" 19 "	Divisional Field day.	
" 20 "	Routine	
" 21 "	Routine	
" 22 "	Routine	
" 22nd	Moved to CAVILLON.	
" 23rd "	Obtained from S Burgoyne informing Division concerning line from CAVILLON to LE QUESNOY	
" 24 "	Routine. Our Battalion both 2" Squadrons at BEAUVOIR	

WAR DIARY
or
INTELLIGENCE SUMMARY.
(Erase heading not required.)

Army Form C. 2118.

Signal Troop
Lucknow Cav. Bde
for month ending 31.x.15

Hour, Date, Place	Summary of Events and Information	Remarks and references to Appendices
Oct 25th CAVILLON	Laid cable to 36th T.H. at OISSY	
" 26 "	Continued above cable through to K.D.G. at MOLLIENS-VIDAMES	
" 27 "	Routine	
" 28 "	Replaced about 400 yds cable in line to Division by over air line	
" 29 "	Routine	
" 30 "	Routine	
" 31 "	Routine.	

SERIAL NO. 239.

Confidential

War Diary

of

Signal Troop, Lucknow Cavalry Brigade.

FROM 1st November 1915 TO 31st December 1915.

Army Form C. 2118.

WAR DIARY
or
INTELLIGENCE SUMMARY.
(Erase heading not required.)

Signal Troop
Lucknow Cavalry Brigade
for month ending 30.XI.15

Place	Date	Hour	Summary of Events and Information	Remarks and references to Appendices
CAVILLON 1.XI.15			Routine - no change	
"	2nd		do	
"	3rd		Started to lay airline to 36th & Jacob's Horse at OISSY, & to K.D.G. at MOLLIENS-VIDAME	
"	4th		Airline continued	
"	5th		do	
"	6th		do	
"	7th		do & communication established	
"	8th		LIEUT. SHEARD I.A.R. with 36th F.A. proceeded on course of instruction (ctr) [?] march/fuel etc. for G.O.C. 3rd Army.	
"	9th		Presentation of french decorations to 2nd Ind. Cav. Div.	
"	9th		Routine - no change	
"	10th		Took in cable previously paid to 36th F.A. & K.D.G.	
"	11th		Routine: no change	
"	12th		do	
"	13th		do	
"	14th		do	
"	15th		do	

Army Form C. 2118.

Instructions regarding War Diaries and Intelligence
Summaries are contained in F.S. Regs., Part II.
and the Staff Manual respectively. Title pages
will be prepared in manuscript.

WAR DIARY
or
INTELLIGENCE SUMMARY.

(Erase heading not required.)

Army Book
followed by Rail
for week ending 30.X.15

Place	Date	Hour	Summary of Events and Information	Remarks and references to Appendices
CAVILLON	16th	—	Routine &c. &c.	
"	17th	—	do.	
VIEULAINE	18th	—	Brigade moved to new billeting area; H.Q. & Signal Troop at VIEULAINE	
"	19th	—	2nd cav. Bde. & R.H.A. at LONGPRÉ & 4th D Squadrons at CONDÉ FOLIE	
"	20th	—	Obliged forward pair of Schüller wires from CHATEAU VIEULAINE to FONTAINE in lieu of 3GB wire at last place	
"	21st	—	Also to 3GB to link H.Q. here from LINE H.Q. at CONDÉ FOLIE to detached squadron at BETTENCOURT withdrawn & terminated now from LONGPRÉ to BETTENCOURT to the house	
"	22nd	—	Single wire from DOMLEGER at LE QUESNOY ENDLOISON fed into H.Q. Signal Office	
"	23rd	—	Routine as above	
"	24th	—	do.	
"	25th	—	do.	
"	26th	—	do.	
"	27th	—	do.	
"	28th	—	do.	
"	29th	—	do.	2 Reviews heard from 2nd Ambulance cannot unjoined
"	30th	—	do.	

Lt. Col. Maitland-Scott
Cmdg. 1st Cav. Bde.
VIEULAINE

Army Form C. 2118.

Instructions regarding War Diaries and Intelligence Summaries are contained in F. S. Regs., Part II. and the Staff Manual respectively. Title pages will be prepared in manuscript.

WAR DIARY
or
INTELLIGENCE SUMMARY.
(Erase heading not required.)

Signal Troop
Lucknow Cav. Bde.
for Month Ending 31.12.15

Place	Date	Hour	Summary of Events and Information	Remarks and references to Appendices
MEERUT	1.12.15		Routine - nothing of E	
"	2 "		do.	
"	3 "		do.	
"	4 "		do.	
"	5 "		do.	
"	6 "		do.	
"	7 "		do.	
"	8 "		do.	
"	9 "		do.	
"	10 "		do.	
"	11 "		do.	
"	12 "		do.	
"	13 "		do.	
"	14 "			
"	15 "		Took in cable to K.D.G. + 2.9th L. preparatory to moving.	

Army Form C. 2118.

Instructions regarding War Diaries and Intelligence
Summaries are contained in F.S. Regs., Part II.
and the Staff Manual respectively. Title pages
will be prepared in manuscript.

WAR DIARY
or
INTELLIGENCE SUMMARY.

(Erase heading not required.)

Place	Date	Hour	Summary of Events and Information	Remarks and references to Appendices
FRANLEU	Dec 16th		Brigade moved into new billeting area. 1/5 & 9 Signal Troop at FRANLEU	
"	17th		1/4 A.F.A. B.D.D.S at LE MONTANT. 1/ f.f.A. at SAIGNEVILLE	
"			Also shot line from FRANLEU across main FRANEVILLE - EU road to connect	
"			to line being laid by R.E. down same road.	
"	18th		Communication established to Div. (Single Div. line) at 6.45 p.m.	
"	19th		Stacey Smith arrived from 14 CAV. Bde.	
"	20th		Routine: Pewit & Lull lamps & 1g & lancers approved his week	
"	21st		Routine: no change	
"	22nd		do	
"			Started by Tac. under black coat in order to obtain minimum	
"	23rd		Routine visual space all day. no wait in keeping signals.	
"	24th		do	
"	25th		do	
"	26th		do	
"	27th		do	
"	28th		do	
"	29th		Bde - visual fog signal Trump - obtained when lights after daylight by	
"			"apt." 4MET LEV 3rd troop	
"	30th		Routine : no change	
"	31st		do	

G.A. Mitchison Capt.
Comdg. Signal Troop 1/9
Lothian + Border Horse

SERIAL NO. 239.

Confidential

War Diary

of

Signal Troop, Lucknow Cavalry Brigade.

FROM 1st July 1916 TO 31st July 1916

Army Form C. 2118.

WAR DIARY or INTELLIGENCE SUMMARY.

Signal Troop, Lucknow Cav Bde.

(Erase heading not required.)

Instructions regarding War Diaries and Intelligence Summaries are contained in F. S. Regs., Part II. and the Staff Manual respectively. Title pages will be prepared in manuscript.

Place	Date	Hour	Summary of Events and Information	Remarks and references to Appendices
CROUCHES	1st		Communication to Bruun by wire "Regts" DR	
	MARCH 2nd		Marched at 6-30 pm to FROHEN-LE-GRAND	
FROHEN-LE-GRAND	3rd		Communication Divion by wire Regts DR	
"	5th		Lines to all units	
"	6th – 14th		Billets	
	MARCH 19th		Marched at 4 am to VILLERS BRULIN 1 motor cyclist, 1 Aiguillette, 2 cyclist orderlies sent forward with two digging party	Messages Total 4691 Maximum 226 Minimum 70
VILLERS BRULIN	20th		Communication to Divn, to D Sqn & 29th Lancers by telephone to 36th & MGS by orderly	
	20 – 30		Routine. Billets.	
	MARCH 31st		Marched to CHELERS. Communication Divn, 36th Jb telephone direct Regts, 29th L telephone thou Divn	

OTC Jackson Cpl.

SERIAL NO. 239.

Confidential
War Diary
of

Signal Troop, Lucknow Cavalry Brigade.

FROM 1st August 1916 TO 31st August 1916.

Army Form C. 2118.

WAR DIARY
or
INTELLIGENCE SUMMARY.

Signal Troop Lucknow Cav. Bde.

(Erase heading not required.)

Instructions regarding War Diaries and Intelligence Summaries are contained in F.S. Regs., Part II. and the Staff Manual respectively. Title pages will be prepared in manuscript.

Place	Date	Hour	Summary of Events and Information	Remarks and references to Appendices
CHELERS	August 1/8/16	—	Communications to all units & telephones direct.	
	1st–5th		Billets, routine.	
	5th–8th		Billets	
	9th		moved to PAS-EN-ARTOIS. Communications through 4th Corps.	Total mms formed 4586
PAS	10th		Line laid to KDGdn. 9th L communication from WARLINCOURT office	Max. 230 Min. 111
	11th		Line laid to 36th Horse. KDG line faults	
	12th		KDG line put right	
	9)&		KDG line extended to COULLEMONT and WARLUZEL. 36th J.H & 29th Rifle Bde. Communication fair.	
	22nd		Replaced enamelled wire with cable. Secret communications Collected cable to 36th J.H. Late sulks in at GAUDIEMPRÉ	good
	23rd		Robotericur on a pair of wires was did not stop communication	and
	24–31st		Billets & routine. Heavy rain gave our troubles with lines for a length of entirely land armed wire was never showed a fault.	good

M A C Dudgeon Capt
Signal Troop

SERIAL No. 239.

Confidential
War Diary
of

Signal Troop, Lucknow Cavalry Brigade.

FROM 1st September 1916 TO 30th September 1916.

Army Form C. 2118.

WAR DIARY
or
INTELLIGENCE SUMMARY.
(Erase heading not required.)

Instructions regarding War Diaries and Intelligence Summaries are contained in F. S. Regs., Part II. and the Staff Manual respectively. Title pages will be prepared in manuscript.

Month: September

Signed Thorp Lockyer Lieut Col_

Place	Date	Hour	Summary of Events and Information	Remarks and references to Appendices
PAS	1st		Communication by wire & all units & to VII Corps	
March	3rd		Marched to OCCOCHES. Cme by DR to all units & Corps	
March	4th		Marched to BRAILLY. Cme by DR to all units & Corps. Hexyrean	
	5th		Cme by phone with Corps 11:10AM — units by DR	
March	11th		Marched to FROHEN-LE-GRAND. Comm by phone, units by DR	
March	12th		Marched to HEM. All cme by DR	
March	13th		Marched to ALLONVILLE. All cme by DR	
March	15th		Marched to area near VILLE-SOUS-CORBIE 4 AM. All cme by DR	
	15/16th		Weather very hot. Roads reconnoitred up to MONTAUBAN	
	18th		Moved Headquarters 1 mile S. E. MORLANCOURT — MÉAULTE road Cme by phone with Corps 3.30 pm.	
	20.01		Routine	
	21st		"	
	22nd		"	
	23rd		"	

E M_ Thompson Capt.

Army Form C. 2118.

WAR DIARY
or
INTELLIGENCE SUMMARY.

(Erase heading not required.)

Signal Troop.
Lucknow Cav. Bde.

Instructions regarding War Diaries and Intelligence Summaries are contained in F.S. Regs., Part II. and the Staff Manual respectively. Title pages will be prepared in manuscript.

September

Place	Date	Hour	Summary of Events and Information	Remarks and references to Appendices
MORLENCOURT	24th		Routine	
	25th		Took over VIA office 6AM	
			On one hours notice from 12noon	
	26th	6AM	Handed over VIA office at 6AM	
		12-45PM	Ordered to move across to MAMETZ with KDGsh	
		2-7PM	Reached MAMETZ	
		2-25PM	Communication up with YU at MONTAUBAN	
		4-30 "	HIP oppo at WATERLOT farm - telephone & 2RE, visual & YU	
		7 "	HIP closed and telephone communication opened with 2RE from MONTAUBAN	
	27th	8AM	Marched to previous billets N. of MORLENCOURT	
		10-30	reopened telephone with VIA.	
		2-30	Closed station, reopened at BUSSY. all cne by DB	
	28th	8AM	Closed BUSSY, reopened HARVEST. all cne by DR	
	29th	10AM	Closed HARVEST, reopened BOIS L'ABBEY. Phone & VIA. Visits by DR	
	30th	9AM	Closed BOIS L'ABBEY 9AM. Reopened at CRECY	

W.A. Thompson Capt.

SERIAL NO. 239

Confidential

War Diary

of

Signal Troop, Lucknow Cavalry Brigade

FROM 1st October 1916 TO 30th November 3rd October 1916.

Army Form C. 2118.

WAR DIARY
or
INTELLIGENCE SUMMARY.

Signal Troop Lucknow Cav. Bde.

(Erase heading not required.)

Octr

Place	Date	Hour	Summary of Events and Information	Remarks and references to Appendices
CRECY	1st	3.30 p.m	Communication with 29th Bde by telephone	
		5.51	Communication with KD9 by telephone	
	2nd	12.30 p.m	Communication with Divn by telephone. Two lines repaired under shell fire	
			Communication good.	
	3rd, 4th, 5th		Built lines.	
	6th		2nd Lt. C.F. Cumberledge KD9 (SR) 15th evg on command, Lieut. Capt Empson F. Dunley	
	7th-8th, 31st		Patrols, maintain	

C.F. Cumberledge 2/Lt

Army Form C. 2118.

WAR DIARY

~~INTELLIGENCE SUMMARY~~ Signal Troop

Lucknow Cav. Bde.

November

(Erase heading not required)

Place	Date	Hour	Summary of Events and Information	Remarks and references to Appendices
CREEY	1st		Routine	
MOYENNEVILLE	2nd	9 AM	Closed CREEY, opened MOYENNEVILLE.	
		4.50 PM	Communication with KDG & 36JH by telegraph & telephone. D3.	
	3rd/4th		Routine	
	5th	8.40 PM	Communication with 1st & 9 CD through MHOW Bde, buzzing only, speaking impracticable owing to noise in line.	
	6th	4.30 PM	Communicated with 29th L. telegraph & telephone. D3.	
	7th/14th		Routine.	
	15th	11 AM	Communicated to ABBEVILLE with Bde telephone & Double current Simplex	
		11.15 AM	— 1st 9 CD — through ABBEVILLE	
		11.30 AM	Line to MHOW Bde dis.	
	16th		Routine	
	17th	3 pm	B Bat. o n.c.o's arrive, 17 Indian & 0 ranks return to Regt. Increase in establishment of Army Signal Service.	
	18th		Routine	
	19th	11 AM	Office closed for 15 mins. during transfer from village to chateau.	
	20th/21st		Routine. Communication through ABBEVILLE to 1st & 9 ED AB	
	22nd/24th		Routine	
	25th		Communication with JODHPUR Lr. by telegraph & telephone. D3.	
	26th/30th	5.30 pm	Routine. ABBEVILLE line guying much trouble since laid owing to contacts.	

C.F. Cambridge 2/Lt.

SERIAL NO. 239.

Confidential
War Diary
of

Signal Troop, Lucknow Cavalry Brigade.

FROM 1st December 1916 TO 31st December 1916.

No. 2.

WAR DIARY.

OF

LUCKNOW CAVALRY BRIGADE SIGNAL TROOP.

For the month of

DECEMBER, 1916.

Army Form C. 2118.

WAR DIARY

INTELLIGENCE SUMMARY.

Signal Troop.
Lucknow Cav. Bde.

December 1916.

(Erase heading not required.)

Instructions regarding War Diaries and Intelligence Summaries are contained in F. S. Regs., Part II. and the Staff Manual respectively. Title pages will be prepared in manuscript.

Place	Date	Hour	Summary of Events and Information	Remarks and references to Appendices
MOYENNEVILLE	1st to 5th	6th.	Bill's Routine.	
	6th.		Communication with VD direct, PIH to AB & VDt AB has joined in ABBEVILLE & AB out of the circuit.	
	7th to 18th		Routine.	
	19th		Lucknow C.J Ambulance at ACHEUX evacuated on to PIH - OBI-JL hrs, Speaking only.	
	20th-31st		Routine.	

C.J Ambulance 2/1/17.